KO MA NE CHI !!

HATSUNE MIKU Presents

Hachune Miku's
Everyday Vocaloid Paradise!

Presented by
ONTAMA
Otomania & Tamago

DO YOUR BEST, MEYKO-SAN

MEYKO-SAN, YOUR BO-YO-YOING IS CRAZY!

EEEH?

MEYKO-SAN, THE BIG SISTER TYPE, HAS A NICE BODY.

COME ON, STOP!

I'M SOOO JEALOUS...

YEAH, AND **AUNTIE'S** JEALOUS, TOO!

BOING

I'M SURE YOURS WILL GET BIGGER!

IF YOU WAIT JUST A LITTLE MORE...

FIDGET

I'M NOT THE MEAN ONE HERE...

THAT'LL TAKE FOREVER!

SO MEAN!

HOW MEAN!

WE HAVE TO WAIT XX YEARS?!

SMACK

I WON'T LOSE TO A SPRING ONION

I'M HA-CHUNE MIKU, THE ELEC-TRONIC FAIRY!

NICE TO MIKU YOU!

> Hachune Miku attacks!

SMACK

I'M KAGUA-MINE RIN!

HEYA!

> Rin parries the Onion Attack!

AAAH!

WHAP

> Len gets caught in the crossfire!

EX-CUSE ME?!

MUNCH

MUNCH

YOU'RE A MON-STER!

> But it wasn't very effective, apparently.

2

CODE NAME: ACT 2

WHAT'S WRONG, MIKU-CHAN?!

WAAAAH!

DASH

I-IT'S RIN! RIN AND LEN ARE...!

RIN-CHAN AND LEN-KUN ARE WHAT?

GRAB

RED LEATHER YELLOW LEATHER RED LEATHER YELLOW LEATHER SHE SELLS SEASHELLS ON THE SEA SHORE

RATTLE RATTLE RATTLE

THE RAIN IN SPAIN STAYS MAINLY IN THE PLAIN PETER PIPER PICKED A PECK OF PICKLED PEPPERS THE RAIN IN SPAIN

THUS, RIN AND LEN WERE UPDATED IN JULY 2008!

RATTLE RATTLE

DO RE MI FA SO

THEY'RE IN REBOOT MODE?!

FLINCH

GASP!

DOUBTS

HI, MIKU-CHAN! YOU'RE CUTE AS EVER~!

KAIYTO-NIISAN LOVES KIDS.

KAIYTO-NIISAN REALLY LOVES KIDS.

THE USUAL CHIPPER RIN-CHAN~!

LEN-KUN!

I'VE GOT SOME ICE CREAM BACK IN MY ROOM~!

KAIYTO-NIISAN REALLY, REALLY LOVES KIDS.

LEN-KYUN, SO CUTE!

SOUNDS KINDA WEIRD.

YUP.

BUT (PROBABLY) ONLY IN A NORMAL WAY.

TO PEEL OR NOT TO PEEL?

WHA--? IS IT?

ACT?

DO SOMETHING ABOUT IT.

RIN-CHAN, YOUR SUNBURN'S PEELING!

AH, THAT'LL DO IT.

GUESS I SWAM AT THE BEACH TOO LONG.

WHOA?

HM?

YEAH-- I PEELED A LOT, TOO!

ARE YOU A SNAKE?!

IDIOT! THAT'S FREAKY!

WHEW!

RE-FRESHED

DRAG DRAG

EEEEK!

CHECK OUT THIS PEEL!

SUMMER TRADITIONS!

SCRAPE

SCRAPE

CRUNCH

CRUNCH

FINALLY DONE!

PHEEEW!

POP

WRONG FRUIT, SEASON, AND COUNTRY.

WHIP

TRICK OR TREAT!

THREE OPTIONS

SPRING ONION!

MOUNTAIN ONION.

WOBBLE

SHIMONITA ONION...!

ALL OF 'EM.

CHOMP

THAT'S ALL THREE.

NOW, WHISH OF THEESH FREE ISH MY FAVORITE?!

DON'T THINK ABOUT IT

YAAAY! LET'S TRY IT!

WOO!

WAT-SAN'S COMPANY SENT US A NEW EBISEN PRODUCT!

CRYPTONITE EBISEN (LTD.)

YEAH, THIS IS ACTUALLY PRETTY GOOD!

YUM! IT'S GOT SPRING ONION IN IT!

UM...

※A MUSIC COMPANY.

JUST WON-DERIN'

WHAT KINDA COMPANY DOES WAT WORK FOR?

BIRTHDAY

THANKS A BUNCH!

HAPPY BIRTH-DAY, RIN-CHAN!

WHA?

HMMM...

DO YA THINK I'VE GROWN A LOT SINCE LAST YEAR?

FIDGET FIDGET

FIDGET FIDGET

YAAAY! GO, RIN-CHAN!

LIAR.

THAT PAUSE SAYS IT ALL.

I SURE DO!

WHAP

IN ONE EAR, OUT THE OTHER

WE'RE HERE!

HOW VALUABLE?

DARN TOOTIN'!

(FAKE KANSAI DIALECT)

BUT JUST BEIN' PUBLISHED ON THE WEB IS LIKE A DREAM, HUH?

YEE-HAW!

(FAKE)

THIS IS A VALUABLE CHANCE, Y'ALL!

HM.

ABOUT AS VALUABLE AS, UH...

THAT'S A WEIRD CHOICE!

THAT MIGHT BE IMPORTANT, BUT...

PUTTING YOUR HANDS ON YOUR HIPS WHEN YOU LINE UP?

BOOP

IMPORTANT ANNOUNCEMENT?

BUT WE HAVE BIG NEWS!

I KNOW THIS IS SUDDEN!

RINRIN HACHUNE

AFTERNOON VOCALOID NEWS →

IS GONNA BE AN ANIME!

HA-CHUNE MIKU...

RINRIN HACHUNE

HAPPY BIRTHDAY, MEYKO-NEESAN

PLEASE LOOK FORWARD TO IT!

PRODUCTION HAS ALREADY BEGUN!

SAVE THOSE KINDA JOKES FOR APRIL!!

IDIOT!

I DID A SEXY SI I DID A ONK SEXY SPRING FOAK OF DANCE OP. FOR THE OP, TOO.

THAT'S THE DREAM I HAD.

WAVE WAVE

● **Hachune Miku Turnaround** ①

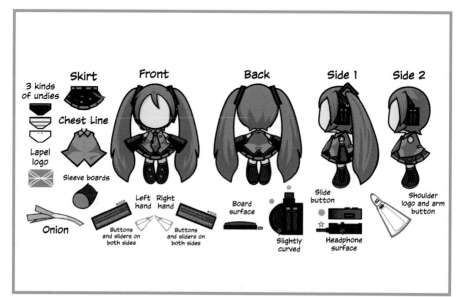

● **Hachune Miku Turnaround** ② (with equipment)

MIKU & RIN

● 2008 New Year's Card

● Christmas Illustration

IN THESE KINDSA ROLES ...?

WHY AM I ALWAYS STUCK...

Comic Market 74 One-Year Congratulatory Illustration

EXTREME VOCALOID

LOIPARA X PIAPRO

A collaborative project with Piapro, the official submission site managed by Crypton Future Media!! We used strict guidelines to choose from the user-submitted illustrations, so here are 20 of the most creative submissions, with comments by Otomania and Tamago!

⬤ ONIONS ARE DELISH ASAYA YUKI-SAN

O: She's just eating spring onions, but I feel like I'm watching the law of the jungle at work.

T: "Survival of the fittest" definitely comes to mind, lol. Miku's so cute, just scarfing them down. But the wriggling spring onion's a little alarming. *Ha ha!*

▶ FLY HIIIGH! SHIMASHINO-SAN

O: H-how can she look so relaxed when she's plummeting at that speed...?

T: She's falling, isn't she? Lol! Wait, it's called "fly high"? I really like the indescribable atmosphere of this one, lol.

⬤ THIS ISN'T A SONG ANYMORE
LEDJOKER07-SAN

O: It looks super strong, but you can also see what seems to be old people dentures in there. Hmm, very deep...

T: A mecha! Awesome, lol. Hard to not comment on the dentures. But it's still super cool! Ha ha!

⬤ DO YOUR BEST AT THE PIANO, MIKU.
AIKU-SAN

O: That piano looks hard! There was an attraction like that at Tokyo Friend Park, I think.

T: It's so heartwarming-- like watching a kid try her best! I wanna rustle her hair and say, "You're so cute!" lol

O: I like how the object's a combo of analog and digital. The colors are very pretty.

T: It's very detailed yet simple, so it's pleasing to the eye. Share some of your art skills with me, please! lol

● COLORFUL BUBBLES
SHIINA UTSUKI-SAN

● AMPLITUDE MODULATION LY
YAWARABI JUUBEE-SAN

O: Everyone's personalities are depicted so cutely. I thought the spring onion was a pipe, lol.

T: The characters inside the bubbles are so lively and cute. Hachune's cute, too, lol.

● KAITO CUP
ABEMERU-SAN
O: If you sucked on the straw, would his face get paler and paler?

T: The thumbnail alone knocked me out--what impact, lol. Can't stop thinking about what would happen once you suck up the contents...

STARTUP ERROR!

IN ORDER TO STARTUP HATSUNE MIKU, PLEASE INSTALL THE "SPRING ONION" PLUGIN.

UNTIL THIS ERROR IS CORRECTED, YOUR SECRET PORN FILES WILL BE DELETED ONE BY ONE.

● HATSUNE VIRUS 2
AKITSUKI RIA-SAN

O: Harsh penalty for not correcting the error. You can really feel the cruel passage of time.

T: The first thing I noticed was the error message-- it cracked me up, lol. Hatsune's expression is perfect, too.

● TROUBLESOME TWINS
MARUSE-SAN

O: There really **are** naughty kids like this. I like how the contents of their graffiti match, too.

T: My kids did the same thing, lol. Kids always draw on the walls, don't they? It's heartwarming and cute.

GRAFFITI: IDIOT WHO ONLY LOVES ICE CREAM / KAITO'S A DUMMY / ICE CREAM
DUMMY / SPRING ONIONS / MEIKO / MIKU / SIS / LEN

● DONDURMA-STYLE KAITO
FUUTO-SAN

O: Turkish ice cream (dondurma) is so stretchy! For some reason, I like how Rin is just smiling like normal.

T: This somehow seems like an accurate depiction of Kaito's role, lol. His expression is just perfect. The kids are cute, too!

● FLOWER MIKU
NIRO-SAN

O: If I got a postcard like this from a friend studying abroad, I'd hang it up forever.

T: It's really lovely. The soft and gentle atmosphere is wonderful. I want to be able to draw pictures like this, lol!

● BOX MIKU
NORANYANKO-SAN

O: This looks like you could actually make it with papercraft. Somebody do it and post it, okay? (lol)

T: I kinda want a person to be inside it, moving it around, lol. Please give us a giant Box Miku, Crypton-sama! Ha ha! a little alarming. Ha ha!

● ORANGE
MOMO☆Y☆A☆-SAN

O: The sorta transparent, round eyes are a great touch--they really draw you in.

T: Those beautiful staring eyes and the tranquility of this one amidst all the energetic submissions really left an impression! ♪

● MEIKO-SAN'S PRECIOUS SAKE-HUNTING SCENE CHIROSUKE-SAN

O: Meiko-san *would* drink that, wouldn't she? ☆ I love the can that's crying "Aahn!"

T: At first, I was like: "Sake (alcohol), sake (salmon)... Oh, I get it!" Took me long enough, lol. She's so desperate. *Ha ha!* It's cute.

EXTREME VOCALOID

● A SCARF CALLED
KAITO NAZO○-SAN

O: More than even the concept, what *really* surprised me was him sitting there so calmly.

T: Is this really a scarf? Or is this just Kaito now? I loled.

● KOKESHILOID
KIYOSHI-SAN

O: The atmosphere is kinda emotional, yet with a strong impact. A mysterious picture.

T: It's very surreal, lol. And solemn, somehow. I bet an old lady would have these by her bed, ha ha.

● KAGAMINE-SAN'S BEWILDERMENT
BASSOU-SAN

O: "Hey, why's it taking pictures of my face? I wanna take pictures of the cat. I don't understand tech these days..."

T: "Hm. So if I press this... Whoops, deleted Kaito-nii's picture. Oh, well."

● VOCALOTIN
NANAKAMI MANA-SAN

O: It's so wonderful that you start to believe there really was a toy like this.

T: The children look like they could come to life any second, and the coloring has the warmth of a picture book--it's fantastic. Their cheeks look so soft, ha ha. Very cute!

CAN: CAT FOOD

● SUCCESSFUL CATCH
TOU CLICK-SAN

O: When you're wearing a scarf, be *extra careful* not to get it caught in your bike wheels or anything, kids...

T: Kaito, run! The mood difference between the captured Kaito and everyone else cracks me up. Len-kun is a good kid.

KAITOFU.

KAITO AND

KAITO

● KAITO AND
TOFU AONO-SAN

← MADE OF TOFU

O: It makes me want to yell, "What the heck?!" Based on the color of that tofu, it'd probably be bad for you. (lol)

T: I didn't notice it was tofu until Otomania-san pointed it out. I couldn't read the title, so I was like, "What's 'mamefu'?" lol alarming. *Ha ha!*

PRESENTED BY

ONTAMA

CONTENTS

spring onion

SPRING ONION 1:
HACHUNE MIKU'S ARRIVAL

IT'S HERE

IT'S COMING

ONE DAY, AT VOCALOID MANOR...

HM? A LETTER FROM THE LAND-LORD-- *THAT'S* UNUSUAL.

Dear Meyko-san:
A newcomer will be delivered to the house today, so please take care of them.

Crypton Wat

DING-DONG

DELI-VERED ?!

ECOLOGY

MY FAVORITE FOOD IS SPRING ONIONS.

YES!

AH HA HA...

YOU'RE SO, UH... SPIRITED! I'M THE **MANAGER**, MEYKO. NICE TO MEET YOU.

BEFORE I SHOW YOU TO YOUR ROOM, ARE YOU HUNGRY?

I GUESS YOU'LL LIVE HERE FROM NOW ON.

I COULD NOT EAT ANOTHER BITE!

NO, THANK YOU!

I SEE.

WHOOF

GREETING

UM... ARE YOU THE "NEW-COMER"?

SHOVE

I'M HA-CHUNE MIKU, THE ELECTRONIC FAIRY!!

NICE TO MIKU YOU!

HGH!

RFF!

FARM-FRESH DELIVERY

AGAIN?

IDENTIFICATION

MANAGER MEYKO

IT'S AN INSTITUTION FOR VOCALOIDS.

THIS IS VOCALOID MANOR. AS ITS NAME IMPLIES...

SPRING ONION 2:

HACHUNE MIKU'S APPETITE

AND DEEPEN OUR BONDS AT THE SAME TIME!

WE ALL WORK HARD AND COOPERATE!

PRETTY AMAZING, RIGHT?!

BISH

WE EVEN HAVE A STUDIO!!

SHE'S DEFINITELY BLUNT.

YEAH, I KNOW.

NEW-COMER'S GUIDE

DUUN

ICE CREAM GOES IN THE FREEZER

CONFESSION

DELICIOUS ANGLES

HMM, HMM.

THEY TASTE BETTER FROZEN! THEY GET ALL **CRUNCHY!**

BUT WHY ARE YOU **FREEZING** THEM?

THE CITY'S SCARY--SO I CAN USE 'EM AS WEAPONS, TOO!

OKAY, BUT... THIS MANY?

WEAP-ONS?

OH, YEAH.

WAIT. IF *YOU'RE* HERE, WHERE'S LEN-KUN?

POKE POKE

HE'S EATIN' IN THE CORNER.

HE LIKES LITTLE SPACES.

MIKU-CHAN!

GAH!

ENCOUNTER

OH, RIN-CHAN.

AH! K... KAIYTO-NII!

SCUTTLE

WHY DO YOU KEEP SCOOTING BACK?

UH, I'M FINE...

H-HOW'VE YOU BEEN?

SHUFFLE

SHUFFLE

KAIYTO-NII, YOU'RE...

I-I MEAN.

MIKU-CHAN, WHAT HAVE YOU BEEN *TELLING* PEOPLE?!

JOLT

A LOLICON, RIGHT?!

I DON'T WANNA GET TOO CLOSE!

BREAKTHROUGH

STARE

?

STARE

PLOP

WHY IN THE HECK ?!

WHA ?!

IT'S RIN-CHAN!!

HOME POSITION

I'M HERE TO PLAAAY!

KAIYTO LOLICON

KAIYTO-N//////!

KWAM

AW, LEN'S SITTIN' IN HIS LAP!

MEEEY-CHAAAN...

GUESS I'LL SIT IN MEY-CHAN'S LAP, THEN!

H-HEY!

23

AFTER DINNER

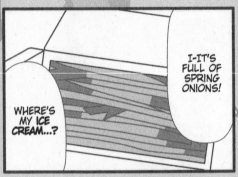

EXTRA

24

IT'S
HOT...

UUUNH...

HACHUNE'S KNOCKED OUT

HUFF... HUFF...

HUFF...

OH...

MIKU-CHAN HASN'T FELT WELL SINCE YESTERDAY.

SPRING ONION 3:
HACHUNE MIKU'S TRANSFORMATION

DO YOU WANT ICE CREAM?

DO YOU NEED ANY-THING?

ONIONS!

REALLY?

HUFF HUFF HUFF...

SPRING ONIONS... N-NEED ONIONS.

UNEXPECTED

HUFF...

TA-DAAA!

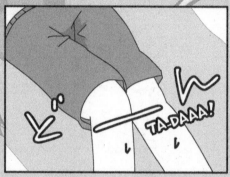

TA-DAAA!

HUH ...?

HUFF... HUFF...

TA-DAAA!

WHAT'S GOING ON WITH YOU?!

I CAN SEE YOUR UVULA...

WHAT IS... GOING ON?

LONG-AWAITED

WE'LL HAVE TO BE CAREFUL.

I CAN'T BELIEVE RUNNING OUT OF SPRING ONIONS WOULD MAKE HER *THAT* SICK...

WHAAAAAAAH?!

HOW'S MIKU-CHA--

I'M HOME!

ARE YOU --?!

WH-WHAT IS IT?!

WHAT?!

LIKE A DRAWING

I'LL HAVE WATER, PLEASE...

CAN YOU EAT THE ONIONS NOW? OR MAYBE SOME **WATER**?

MIKU-CHAN, TEA TOWEL!

KYAAAA!

SPLSSH

AH!

WHAP

SHE'S SICKLY AN' CLUMSY? WHAT KINDA MOE CHARACTER IS SHE?!

NOOO!

KYAAAA!

KRRRASH

CLANG

WHP

WHY

TWEET

TWEET

OKAY, GOT IT.

YOU GREW **BIGGER** BECAUSE YOU RAN OUT OF SPRING ONIONS?

WELL, WHAT CAN YOU DO?

SO, THAT MAKES YOU GET BIGGER, HUH?

HEY! DO THEY NOT NOTICE HOW **WEIRD** THIS IS?!

OH, WELL.

AH HA HA HA!

♪

FLAP

BIG BROTHER!

CATCHING HEARTS

HOPES AND DREAMS

FRESH-SQUEEZED

SPRING ONION REMEDY

DREAMS AND REALITY

HACHUNE MIKU

THE SPRING ONION-WAVING, IGNORANCE-FEIGNING HEROINE!

Hachune Miku is the official, maker-approved SD version of Hatsune Miku and the heroine of LoiPara. Her trademarks are spring onions and the spirals on her cheeks. She has a rather sharp tongue and likes to play dumb.

LIKES ALL KINDS OF SPRING ONIONS!

She just really likes spring onions. She was even delivered to the Vocaloid manor in a box of spring onions. She knows all about the different subspecies.

HAS A KILLER SPECIAL MOVE.

She uses a spring onion as a sword for her finishing move in the RPG. She also casts a spell to summon a huge monk called "Onion Lama."

"I'M HACHUNE MIKU, THE ELECTRONIC FAIRY!"

TRANSFORMS INTO A GROWN-UP VERSION?!

When she doesn't get enough spring onions, she transforms into adult Miku. In this form, she's gentle and beautiful. Even just the shock of having no spring onions can make her transform.

TRADITION

TIME FOR A **FLOWER VIEWING** MEETUP!

DA-DAAA!

IN VOCA-LOID MANOR TRADI-TION...

WOO?

WOO!

LET'S SAVE A SPOT THE DAY BEFORE!

YAY! THEN...

WITH MIKU-CHAN THIS YEAR, WE'LL NEED A GOOD SPOT!

HOORAY~!

WHO SHOULD HOLD THE SPOT...?

OKAY.

HMM.

I KINDA **FIG-URED.**

YEAH...

STARE

MUNCH MUNCH

SINCE IT'S OVER-NIGHT.

SPRING ONION 4:
HACHUNE MIKU'S FLOWER VIEWING

FLOWER VIEWING DUMPLINGS

DUMP-LINGS, OF COURSE!

HUH?

MEY-CHAN, WHATCHA **MAKIN'**?

O O O H !

I THOUGHT I'D PUT EVERY-ONE'S FAVORITE FOODS INSIDE. ♥

HUH...?

WE GONNA PLAY **RUSSIAN ROULETTE** WITH THESE?

THIS ONE'S SPRING ONION, THIS ONE'S ORANGE, THAT'S...

WHOA, AWE-SOME! ♥

ESTABLISHED REALITY

HUH?

EVEN IF WE PLAYED FOR IT, IT'D **STILL** BE KAIYTO-NII.

WHAT IS IT?

KAIYTO-NII!!

WATCH, I'LL **PROVE** IT.

SCIS-SORS!!

HUH?!

ROCK, PAPER...

I SEE!

HM, YEAH.

HE'S **SUPER** BAD AT THAT.

SEE?

SOB SOB SOB

35

SURVIVAL OF THE FITTEST

WHERE'S KAIYTO-KUN?

THE NEXT DAY.

RESERVED FOR VOCALOID

GRRRR! <STAY AWAY!>

VOCALO ICE CREAM

HISSSS! <GIMME BACK MY ICE CREAM!>

IT'S WAY TOO EARLY FOR WHAT-EVER THIS IS!

GRRRR!

HISSSS!

HOP

HOP

SPIDER-MAAAN?!

RELIEF SUPPLIES

YES, SIR! I'LL BE BACK SOON!

KAIYTO-KUN'S ALL ALONE. CAN YOU BRING HIM SUP-PLIES?

OH, THANK YOU!

I BROUGHT YOUR SUPPLIES, COLONEL!

WHY "COLO-NEL"?

BRRR, SO COLD...

ZWOOOSH

WHAT'D YOU BRING M--

NOGGIN

BRRRRR...

WITH PLENTY OF DRY ICE!

YOUR FAV-ICE CREAM!

NOM NOM

LEN'S AWAKENING

TASTY DELICACY

BLACKED OUT

HOW OBLIVIOUS CAN HE GET?!

THAT STUPID KAIYTO-KUN.

I-I'VE GOT CHARMS, TOO! SOOO MANY CHARMS...

I KNOW KAIYTO-KUN MIGHT BE A LOLICON, BUT...

WHAT'S SHE SAYING TO LEN-KUN?

RANT RANT

FLOWER VIEWING AND SAKE

THEY REALLY ARE.

IN FULL BLOOM, HUH?

YES. ME, TOO...

POP

I'M GLAD WE GOT TO SEE THEM TO-GETHER.

AH HA HA!

CRACK

IT'D BE NICE IF BIG MIKU-CHAN WAS HERE.

THAT'S IMPOSSIBLE, THOUGH.

WHAT A MORON...

GLUG GLUG GLUG GLUG

BOY, YOU'RE REALLY DRINK-ING...

UM.

HAPPY TIMES

CAT ENCOUNTER

WELCOME TO THE DIGITAL WORLD

WAT-SAN ASKED US TO TEST OUT A NEW RPG MACHINE!

TA-DAA~! ♪

SPRING ONION 5:
HACHUNE MIKU'S ADVENTURE

WE'RE GOIN' IN A SIM?

WHOA...

YUP!

PUT THEM ON YET?

MUNCH MUNCH

WOOO!!

ALL RIGHT-- OFF TO THE RPG WORLD!

TYPICAL MEYKO-SAN.

WOW...

TEE HEE ♥

BY THE WAY, WHAT'S AN RPG?

THE NOBLE PATH

SPECIAL ATTACK

*From Tokimeki Memorial, a series of dating sim games from Konami.

BLACKED OUT

INSTANT SUMMONS

42

OUT WITH A BANG

THE FINAL BOSS AND ME

THE FIGHT ENDS

THE DOOR AIN'T EX-ACTLY SCARY.

WE MADE IT! I HOPE KAIYTO-KUN'S OKAY.

'SCUSE ME!

BARGIN' IN, HUH?

WHAM

YEAH, TO-TALLY!

HEE HEE!

TREE OF LEGEND

YOU CALL 'EM "GIRLS" TILL X GRADE, RIGHT?

AH HA HA!

WANNA JOIN US FOR ICE CREAM?

HUH? HEY, GUYS-- WHAT'S UP?

RRRUUUURRRR

THE ULTIMATE SPELL

YEAH, TRUE.

HIII-YA!

WHACK

MIKU-NEE! THERE'S NO END TO THESE GUYS!

WHAP

WHY'D YOU KEEP IT A SECRET?!

I'LL HAVE TO USE MY SECRET ULTIMATE SPELL.

DU

UN!!

MUNCH MUNCH

ULTI-MATE SPELL... ONION LAMA!

YAAH!

SMACK

NOOOO! DON'T EAT MY PRE-CIOUS ONIONS!!

EPILOGUE

FINAL BATTLE

KAGUAMINE RIN

THE WISE-CRACKING PEPPY GIRL! ♥

Kaguamine Rin is the SD version of Rin, one of the Kagamines from the second installment in the Vocaloid series. She speaks in a Kansai dialect for some reason, cracking jokes and making comebacks at just the right moment. Her favorite thing is oranges.

She plays straight man to the many weirdos of the Vocaloid group. She and Miku are just like a stand-up comedy duo.

......

THAT THERE'S *MASOCHISM*, PERV!!

HA HA HA!

NERU-KUN'S SCOLDING IS THE *BEST MOE*, OUI OUI!

THE SNACK-LOVING KANSAI GAL!

As her Kansai dialect implies, she loves Kansai foods like takoyaki and okonomiyaki, and can be very annoying about it. Maybe it's in her Osakan blood?

URYYYYYY!!

TAKOYAKIIIIII!

WHY IN THE HECK—?!

TRANSFORMS WITH ORANGES?!

THEN, MAYBE I'LL GET 20% BIGGER ALL OVER?!

Just like Miku, if her body doesn't get enough oranges, she'll transform--or so we thought. Nobody has ever seen it happen, though. Maybe she's deluding herself?!

FIRST MEETING

AH!

TAKE THIS!

NOOO, COME BACK!

DOING   DOING

I'M THE WEIRDO?!

AAAH! A WEIRDO!!

HEY, LOLICON!

SPRING ONION 6:
HACHUNE MIKU'S OPEN HOUSE, SIDE A

I KNEW IT

OH!!

I'M HACHUNE MIKU, THE ELECTRONIC FAIRY!

?

HM?

WHISPER WHISPER

AND THIS IS...

AHA!

TH-THAT'S NOT--!

NOOO.

HE IS **LOLICON** FREAK...

...EH?

OH, A FAD DIETER!

WRONG ON **SO** MANY LEVELS.

SHORT FOR **CALORIE CONTROL**!!

RESTRICTED AREA

SWEET ANN!

MY NAME IS ANN!

STAY BACK!

WH-WHO **ARE** YOU?! WHAT ARE YOU DOING HERE?

OOOH!

HUH?

I AM MESSENGER OF JUSTICE, PROTECTING PEACE!

OH, SHE'S NORMAL?

AAAH!

BY DAY, I AM SINGING INSTRUCTOR!

TAP

NOPE, NOT NORMAL.

AMAZING!

BUT BY NIGHT, I AM **PROTECTING PEACE** IN THIS PARK!

I AM FINE

A SELF-PROCLAIMED ALLY OF JUSTICE.

AHEM! THIS IS ANN-SAN.

GLEAM GLEAM

N-NICE TO...

NICE TO MEET YOU!

UM... <PLEASED TO MEET?>

OH! REALLY?

I PURSUE CAREER AS VOCALOID.

BY DAY...

WHY ARE YOU CRYING?!

AND BY NIGHT... I PROTECT PEACE IN PARK... SNIFF.

NOW YOU'VE DONE IT

ENOUGH ALREADY...

OKAY, SO IT'S REALLY LOLITA COMPLEX.

HMM?

OH, MEYKO-SAN.

WHAT'RE YOU DOING IN THE PARK?

WHA--?!

SHOVE

HIII-YAH!!

WH-WHAT, ANN-SAN?!

JAPANESE BOYS CAN BE ASSER-TIVE. ♡

OH!

AHA!

MEYKO-SAN!

GAH!

DASH

A REAL ADULT

THAT'S NOT WHAT IT MEANS... AND IT'S NOT JAPANESE.

"YOU CAN'T TAKE IT WITH YOU."

THERE IS EVEN JAPANESE SAYING ABOUT THIS.

HUH?! WHAT'S WRONG?!

COLLAPSE

GROOOOOWWWL

I THINK SHE'S HUNGRY.

MAIN POWER SUPPLY DRAINED... BACK-UP POWER OFFLINE...

I'M AN ADULT

REVIVED

THEN WHY THE PARK...?

I AM SINGING TEACHER AT MUSIC SCHOOL BY TRAIN STATION.

AND THAT OUTFIT IS A **BIT** MUCH.

SNIFFLE

ALWAYS DREAM TO GO TO JAPAN.

YOU SEE, I LOVE JAPANESE CULTURE.

AND PLACE I MOST WANTED TO GO TO LEARN ABOUT JAPAN...

RUMMAGE

RUMMAGE

WHAT A WEEB.

AHA~! JAPAN IS THE BEST!

COLONEL! THERE'S A HUGE STASH OF FIGURES AND MANGA IN HERE!!

VISITOR

FINALLY, AN ADULT

LET'S GET ALONG

A FIRST

MOVING

OOOH!

THANK YOU FOR HAVING ME, EVERYONE!

OLDER LADY TALK.

YOU'RE MAKING ME BLUSH!

I AM LUCKY TO MEET SUCH LOVELY PEOPLE!

HEE HEE.

WHERE'S YOUR LUGGAGE?

BY THE WAY...

ARE YOU A ONE-LADY ANIME CON?

WHAT?

THIS IS ALL OF IT.

Kochi Oranges

ONION!

THAT'S ALL?!

WOW!

HOBBIES AND INTERESTS

ANN-SAN, WHERE DID YOU LEARN JAPANESE?

WHERE DID I LEARN?

LET ME SEE...

MOSTLY FROM JAPANESE MANGA!

THEY ARE SOLD IN MANY PLACES.

WHAT'S YOUR IMAGE OF JAPAN, THEN?

WABI-SABI! HARAKIRI! MOE!

MOE IS VERY POPULAR OVERSEAS!

THAT'S A BIT ONE-SIDED.

FAVORITE JAPANESE SINGERS?

ICHIROU! AKIRA! HIRONOBU!

THEY GET ME PUMPED!

POINT

YEAH, I FIGURED.

COMMON KNOWLEDGE

I KNOW MANY FACTS ABOUT JAPAN!

YEAH?

LIKE... SAMURAI WEAR KATANA ON LEFT!

I-IS THAT SO?

IF THEY WORE THEM ON RIGHT, SHEATHS MIGHT HIT WHILE WALKING, LEAD TO SWORD FIGHT.

GRRR

HEY, YOU!

CLINK

THAT IS WHY THEY DRIVE ON LEFT IN JAPAN. SO BE CAREFUL OF SWORD FIGHTS, OKAY?

WHAT CENTURY ARE THESE FACTS FROM...?

EH HEH HEH.

HAIR'S BREADTH

TH-THAT'S GOOD...

THESE THINGS HAPPEN.

THEY UNDERSTOOD WHEN I EXPLAIN.

I DON'T THINK THOSE WERE COSPLAYERS.

I WAS GLAD FOR NICE COSPLAYERS!

AHA

IF THEY DID NOT LISTEN...

BECAUSE...

NO! YOU CAN'T RESORT TO VIOLENCE!!

MAYBE IT WOULD HAVE BEEN "NICE BOAT*" SITUATION!

TEE HEE!

PILGRIMAGE

OH NO, DID SOMETHING **HAPPEN**?

BUT THERE ARE STRANGE PEOPLE IN **JAPAN**, TOO!

SUCH SPIRIT.

TO SACRED SITE!

MY FIRST DAY HERE, I WENT STRAIGHT...

SO, SO MUCH SPIRIT.

THERE, I FOUND MOUNTAIN OF TREASURES! I WENT **WILD**!

THAT'S NOT COS-PLAY!

DUUN

THANK YOU FOR YOUR SERVICE.

BUT WHEN DANCING, I WAS SURROUNDED BY POLICE COSPLAYERS.

*Japanese meme from 2007. Due to an incident the day before it aired, the violent finale of School Days was replaced with scenery footage, including a Norwegian ferry, prompting the comment, "nice boat."

SHIPPING

GOOD FRIENDS

HELLO AGAIN

HUH? WE'RE OUT OF ONIONS.

THE NEXT MORNING.

EMPTY

AH!

WE ATE THEM LAST NIGHT WHILE DRINKING, I'LL GO BUY--

OH, I'M SORRY!

BUY GROCERIES

YOUR SPRING ONION LEVEL HIT ZERO ALREADY?!

O-OH. UM...

UH-OH...

UH... THIS LOOKS BAD.

TWING

TWING

TWING

OTP

YEAH, I AM.

ARE YOU DRINKING?

A MAN AND WOMAN, REALLY CLOSE?

MEY-SAN AND NII-SAN, ARE YOU LIKE THAT?

HOO HOO.

SURE, WE'RE CLOSE! MEYKO-SAN'S A BIG HELP!

WH-WHAT?!!

BLUSH!

NAH, HE'S JUST THAT STUPID.

HE DOES ON PURPOSE?

OW, OW, OW!

GRR!

58

REAL MOE

MORNING...

WHA--?!

GOOD MORN--

UH-OH. WE'D BETTER BUY SOME QUICK--

I THOUGHT IT'D BE OKAY TO GET MORE THIS MORNING.

I FINISHED THE SPRING ONIONS LAST NIGHT.

KAIYTO-SAAAN!

WHERE ARE MIKU-CHAN AND ANN-SAN?

THEY WERE RIGHT HERE.

MUURRRR...

WELL... YEAH.

IT SUITS HER! PERFECT!

WHAT DO YOU THINK? VERY MOE, NO?

UMM...

EH HEH!

VERY EXCITED

YESSSSSS!!

KYAAH?!

AAH! SOME-ONE HELP!

MIKU-SAN, YOU BECOME SO BIG! YOU CAN TRANSFORM? WONDERFUL!

EXPLAIN?

YOU SEEM SURPRISED, SO LET ME EXPLAIN.

WAAH!

MUTTER

GOOD ENOUGH.

RAWR!

NO NEED! IT IS BECAUSE SHE IS MAGICAL GIRL, YES?!

IT'S NOT GOOD AT ALL! WAAH...

KAGUAMINE LEN

THE QUIET, BANANA-LOVING BOY.

An SD version of Kagamine Len.
In this manga, he and Rin seem to be twins? He's usually just spaced out, or sitting in the corner eating something. His favorite thing is bananas.

SILENT CHARM

He hasn't spoken once in the entire manga so far. Despite his lack of lines, he's charmed lots of people with his cute, round eyes.

THEY SAY HIS SMILE'S AMAZING...

He's always staring into space, but the smile he occasionally shows the other Vocaloids (but never the readers) captures all their hearts.

NERU THINKS HE'S HOT?!

Akita Neru fell in love with Len at first sight when he picked up her phone. From her perspective, he's a stunningly handsome boy... Is she delusional?!

GIANT ANTEATER

AH.

OH, I WAS JUST THINKING.

WHAT'S UP, MIKU-NEE?

HUH?

ABOUT GIANT ANTEATERS.

SPRING ONION 7:
HACHUNE MIKU'S DILEMMA

THE FOOD CHAIN CONTINUES

ON TOP OF THAT?

A-AND ON TOP OF THAT!

IF THERE WAS A *REALLY BIG* KIND OF GIANT ANTEATER-EATER...

RUMBLE

A GIANT, GIANT ANT-EATER-EATER!

THEN THAT'D HAVE TO BE...

YOU'RE ON A DANGER-OUS ROAD THERE.

CALM DOWN, BUDDY.

AND THEN... IF SOME-THING ATE THOSE...

HUFF... HUFF...

THE FOOD CHAIN

GIANT ANTEATER.

UH-HUH.

THE THINGS WITH THE LONG, THIN FACES?

UH, YOU *JUST* REALIZED THAT?

I JUST REALIZED THEY'RE CALLED ANTEATERS 'CAUSE THEY EAT ANTS...

POINT

DON'T POINT THAT THING AT PEOPLE.

SO, I WAS **THINKING**, LIKE...

TWIRL TWIRL

· · · · · · ·

IF THERE WAS AN ANIMAL THAT ATE **THEM**, WOULD IT BE A GIANT ANTEATER-EATER?

CUTE

GIANT ANT-EATERS?

HMM?

MEY-CHAN DOESN'T KNOW?

QUICK TO SAY SORRY, *HUH?* OKAY.

SORRY.

I DON'T KNOW MUCH ABOUT THEM.

FROM THEIR LONG SNOUTS TO THEIR *SQUIGGLY* TONGUES!

BUT GIANT ANT-EATERS ARE *ADORABLE*, HUH?

THOSE FACES!

SHE'S S'POSED TO BE AN **ADULT**.

MEYKO-SAN'S THE CUTE ONE, HUH?

OH, SO CUTE!

PWHAAH.

A MATURE ADULT

MIKU

MAYBE YOU SHOULD ASK AN ADULT 'BOUT THAT?

YEAH! YOU'RE SO SMART, RIN-CHAN!

CREEEAK

I'LL GO TO MEY-CHAN'S ROOM N--

ASK ME ANY-THING YOU LIKE!

AN **ADULT**, YOU SAY?!

......

HEY, MEYKO-SAN!

MEY-CHAAAN!

EVERYONE'S HEARTS

NO, NO!

MAYBE YOU ARE NOT **JUST** PERVERT!

KAIYTO-SAN KNOWS **A LOT**, YES?

HEE HEE.

YOU CAN COUNT ON ME!

I HAVE A QUESTION FOR KAIYTO-NIISAN, TOO!

DO YOU UNDERSTAND A WOMAN'S HEART?!

DOON

HERE GOES!

THAT'S NOT 'BOUT ANIMALS!

LIIIES!

OF COURSE I DO!

ABSO-LUTELY!

DEEP FEELINGS

ABOUT GIANT ANT-EATERS.

OH?

BUT THEY'RE CALLED **JAGUARS** AND **PUMAS**, NOT GIANT ANTEATER-EATERS!

THERE **ARE** SOME BIG CATS THAT EAT THEM...

IT DIGS INTO THEIR NESTS WITH ITS SHARP CLAWS.

ALSO, THE GIANT ANTEATER MOSTLY EATS **TERMITES!**

WHOA.

UH-HUH, UH-HUH.

WOW!

OOH!

HERE'S THE DIMWIT

WELL, THE DIMWITTED MAN IS A PROBLEM...

BUT SHE SHOULD ALSO **SPEAK** HER FEELINGS!

IF SHE LOVES THIS DIMWIT, SHE HAS TO BE MORE PROACTIVE!

STAB

SHE HAS TO BELIEVE IN HERSELF!

STAB

WOBBLE

CLENCH

MORE LIKE IGNORANCE IS A **SIN**.

STAB

STAB

IGNORANCE IS BLISS, *HUH?*

ACTRESS

MEN ARE THE **WORST**.

OKAY?

YES, YOU LADY-KILLER! NEXT QUESTION!

OWWW...

BUT MAN IS **VERY DENSE** AND DOES NOT SEE.

A WOMAN IS SECRETLY IN LOVE WITH MAN.

"OH, ONLY **ALCOHOL** CAN COMFORT."

"WHY HE DOESN'T NOTICE MY FEEL-INGS?"

TRACE

TRACE

TRACE

OOOOH!

DRIED SQUID IS BEST DRINKING SNACK OF ALL!

EMERGENCY SITUATION

ACTUAL SIZE

THE WHOLE HOUSE

VOCALOID MANOR.

HACHUNE MIKU'S SHOPPING TRIP

IT'S NICE OUT. MAYBE THE DE-PARTMENT STORE?

I NEED SOME HOUSE THINGS.

OF COURSE YOU CAN!

I WANT A FEW THINGS. CAN I COME?

H-HUH?

68

WHAT A BARGAIN

OH!

SNATCH

THESE WERE SOLD OUT EVERY-WHERE!!

AAAH! HIKYOU SENTAI URO-TANDER CARDS!

AND SUPER-RARE KEYBOARD CRUSHER 1/8TH FIGURE!

I AM HAPPIEST EVER!

'CAUSE SHE'S A **BIG** KID.

WOW, LOTS OF TOYS.

I WILL TAKE IT ALL, PLEASE!

CASHIER

HOMETOWN

Sign: Otomanishop

OOH! *THIS IS A* DEPART-MENT STORE?!

YOU'VE NEVER SEEN ONE?

AH.

MY OLD TOWN JUST HAD A SPRING ONION FIELD.

THEN ANOTHER ONION FIELD...

AND PAST THAT, AN-OTHER.

WITH *THAT* FACE? NAH.

MAYBE SHE'S **HOME**-SICK?

SPRING ONIONS TO INFINITY... YUMM...

HANDMADE

A GENTLEMAN ALWAYS (ETC.)

BIG FAN

CHILDREN AT PLAY

SUMMERTIME

IF NEXT MONTH WE COULD HELP AT THE BEACH HOUSE, VOCALO.

OH, RIGHT! WAT-SAN ASKED...

YAAAY!!

SHOULD WE BUY SWIMSUITS WHILE WE'RE HERE?

DON'T BE STUPID!

I WANT A BIKINI!

STAAARE

MAYBE... I SHOULD BUY A SWIMSUIT.

MUMBLE

LEN-KYUN

LEN-KUUUN! WHERE AAAARE YOOOU? LEN-KYUN!

LEEEN!

HUH?

I'D BETTER GO.

THROUGH HER EYES.

MY NAME'S LEN.

SHFF

HIS NAME IS LEN-KYUN.

WOW...

MEYKO

EVERYONE'S DEPENDABLE BIG SISTER

Modeled after MEIKO, the female Vocaloid who was released before Miku and Rin/Len. She's a sensible big sister figure who looks after everyone. Secretly in love with Kaiyto.

THE MEDIATOR

AND DEEPEN OUR BONDS AT THE SAME TIME!

WE ALL WORK HARD AND COOPERATE!

Meyko is essentially the manager of Vocaloid Manor. She takes the lead in conversations and looks after Miku, Rin, and Len.

LOVES SAKE!

MYEW! ♥

BWAAAH...

Meyko usually has her act together, but she's actually a big drinker (One Cup sake is her favorite). She's also a bit of a fighting drunk, too... Is she an old man at heart?!

"BRING ON THE SAKE!"

MAN DROUGHT

IN LOVE WITH KAIYTO. ♥

THANK YOU, KAIYTO-KUN.

I'M SO HAPPY!

She secretly has feelings for Kaiyto, but everyone knows except him (lol). Her lovestruck maiden's smile will make your heart pound!

TO THE BEACH HOUSE

(SPRING ONION) LOVER EP.

REUNION

THIS HELPER'S GETTING HER BEARINGS, TOO.

BEAR WITH ME WHILE I INTRODUCE YOU!

LOVES WOMEN

N-NICE TO MEET YOU.

SHE'S AKITA NERU-KUN.

HELLO.

BEARY NICE.

BLANK GLANCE GLANCE

VOCALO BEACH HOUSE

HELLO, I'M MEYKO.

WELL, YEAH? WE JUST MET!

I DIDN'T GET THIS JOB 'CAUSE YOU'D BE HERE!

I DON'T KNOW YOU AT ALL!

AND THIS IS--

TSUNDERE

YESTERDAY'S ENEMY IS TODAY'S (ETC.)

HELLO THERE!

STEAMED BUNS?

WHAT'S THIS...?

GOOD MORNING! WAT-SAN SENT US.

WHA?!

THANKS FOR COMING ALL THIS WAY--

SHUFFLE

VOCALO BEACH HOUSE

HMM?

HUH?

YOU'RE A FRIEND OF WAT-SAN'S?

DON'T GLARE! I CAN'T BEAR IT!

N-NO? YOU DON'T LOOK BEARY FAMILIAR!

HAVE WE MET?

VOCALO BEACH

THANK YOU

MEETING

A LITTLE SLIP-UP

FIRST...

EYE OF THE BEHOLDER

BLANK

...

DON'T LOOK AT ME LIKE THAT.

GLANCE

H-HEY.

BLANK

WE PICKED UP ANOTHER WEIRDO.

SHOVE

I-I'M NOT GONNA GIVE YOU THIS!

SOLILOQUY

STAAARE

SPLSH

SPLSH

BA-DUMP

YOU DON'T WANT TO PLAY, NERU-SAN?

I-I GUESS I COULD IF HE WANTS, BUT...

WHY SHOULD I PLAY WITH LEN-KYUN?!

O-OKAY, JUST DON'T CRY!

SNIFFLE

BE HONEST, OR YOU'LL REGRET IT. IF ONLY I'D BEEN HONEST BACK THEN...

SHALL WE?

<HEY!> YOU GUYS!

WE ARE HERE TO PLAY!

SPRING ONION 10:
HACHUNE MIKU'S TEST OF COURAGE

TA-DA!

TEST OF COURAGE GUIDE-BOOK

WANNA DO A TEST OF COURAGE?

OH HO.

YOU'RE SO PRE-PARED.

THERE'S A FLASHLIGHT AND BUG SPRAY, TOO.

OOH, I'M SO EXCITED!

HEE HEE.

AAH, SO THAT'S IT.

AND FIRE-WORKS... AND A WATER GUN...

BOYS DROOL

FEELINGS THAT WON'T REACH

IN PAIRS

THIS AGAIN

HEH! NOW I CAN GO SCARE THEM!

THE TEST STARTS NOW! WE'LL GO AHEAD!

SALUTE

HERE'S YOUR COSTUME.

HOW BEARY EXCITING! WHAT IS IT?!

PUT IT ON.

NO LITTERING

SHRINE OF LEGEND

SIGH...

OBLIVIOUS

CHATTER

CHATTER

CHATTER

CHATTER

CHATTER

HM.

AH, JEEZ.

GUESS WE'RE ENDIN' UP TOGETHER.

PAFF

NOT EVEN CLOSE! LISTEN, WILL YA?

ANN-SAN, **HOW** OLD ARE YOU?

"TEST OF COURAGE" IS LIKE GHOST-BUSTERS, NO?!

THIS IS IT

ROAR

THIS AGAIN

FIRED UP

TEST OF COURAGE

WISH GRANTED

KAIYTO

THE HAND-SOME BUT STUPID BIG BROTHER.

Modeled after the male Vocaloid KAITO. Like Meyko, he's a good older sibling to Miku, Rin, and Len. He's handsome, but a total idiot who's oblivious to Meyko's feelings for him.

IS HE A LOLICON?!

THEN HOW ABOUT *THIS!*

THIS DO IT FOR YOU, LOLICON?

AAH! YOU WIN!!

THROB

He's been very affectionate toward Miku since they met, leading her to label him a lolicon. Apparently, he just likes kids, both boys and girls.

He loves all kinds of ice cream and will eat it all year long. It might be a little weird for an adult to love ice cream, but you can't help what you like. Just be careful of cavities!

ICE CREAM FOR EVERY SEASON.

ERRRRR...

WITH PLENTY OF DRY ICE!

YOUR *FAV*-- ICE CREAM!

NOM NOM

"IT'S ALWAYS A GOOD TIME FOR ICE CREAM."

Locust Ice Cream

Caviar Flavor

HIS SCARF IS HIS TRADEMARK.

HUH?

IT'S JUST *WHO I AM!*

A SCARF MARKS A *TRUE* GENTLE-MAN!

Kaiyto's signature item is his scarf, to the point where you can't think of him without thinking of scarves--and vice versa. He's even been known to wear a scarf with no shirt...

FESTIVE FEELING

JAPANESE SUMMER FESTIVAL?! EXCITING!

THERE'S A FESTIVAL TODAY!

STILL AT VOCALO BEACH HOUSE.

WH-WHAT ARE YOU **TALKING** ABOUT?!

LUCKY BREAK, NO?

MEY-SAN, YOU GO WITH KAIYTO-SAN.

BA-DUMP!

SLIDE

I-I DON'T HAVE ANY FEELINGS FOR KAIYTO-KUN--

WHAT'S UP, MEYKO-SAN?

AH WAH WAH!

MOU-MANTAI!*

DO NOT WORRY, HE HEARD NOTHING!

I'M GOING SHOPPING, 'KAY?

AAAAH!

*"No problem" in Cantonese, made famous to many otaku in Digimon.

SUNTAN

I PICKED UP SOME STUFF AT THE SHOP.

I'M BACK!

RUSTLE

OH, DO I?

I MEAN, I THINK WE *ALL* DO.

YOU HAVE QUITE A **TAN** NOW, NO?

PLOP

HEY! I WON'T LOSE!

WHA-CHA THINK? **SEXY**, RIGHT?

WOO HOO~!

HOO HOO!

TWIRL

PEEK

A SCARF TAN LINE?! YOU GOTTA BE *KIDDIN'*!

HAVE SOME SELF-RESPECT, BUDDY!!

LOOK. **I'VE** GOT TAN LINES, TOO!

SLIP

LEGEND: PART 3

AGAIN? HOW MANY LEGENDS *IS* THAT, TWENTY-SEVEN?

THERE'S A BEARY **FAMOUS** LEGEND ABOUT THIS FESTIVAL.

MEN + WOMEN

IF A COUPLE WATCHES THE FIREWORKS THERE, THEIR LOVE WILL BEAR FRUIT.

I DON'T KNOW BEAR IT IS, THOUGH.

THERE'S A SECRET PLACE ON A HILL WITH A GREAT VIEW. THEY SAY...

TWITCH

BACK TA WORK.

BUT IT'S **TRUE**, I BEAR!

'KAY, THAT'S ENOUGH LEGENDS FOR **ONE** LIFETIME.

....

FIRE-WORKS, HUH?

....

MUMBLE

91

OUTSIDE THE BOX

WHAT, GOT AN IDEA?

A NORMAL TAKOYAKI SHOP'S BORING.

IT'S THE NEXT BIG THING!!

PICTURE IT! MAID TAKO-YAKI!

POINT

♡ CHU

OOH! GOOD THINKIN'!

I'VE EVEN PREPARED OUTFITS!

GONNA SEE THAT IN MY NIGHT-MARES.

I MADE ONE FOR THE MANAGER, TOO!

PLEASE STOP.

BURNING OSAKAN BLOOD

OH HO. WHAT'LL YOU SELL?

CLENCH

SPARKLE

AND OUR SHOP'LL BE AT THE FESTIVAL, BEAR NONE!

TA...

GLINT

TAKOYAKI THE BEARY BEST!

URYYYYYYY!!

TAKOYAKIIIIII!!

FROO

MAKIN' MY OWN LEGEND, STARTIN' TONIGHT!!!

I'M BURNIN' UP!! I'M ON FIRE!!!

FOOAR

GRAND OPENING

YAAAAY!

YOU'LL GET BREAKS SO EVERY-BEARY CAN ENJOY THE FESTIVAL!

CHAOS

YOU DON'T MISS A BEAT!

I *EVEN* HAVE YUKATA PRE-BEARED!

FULL SPEED AHEAD

TA-

DAAA!

TIME FOR THE BIG REVEAL!!

LOTTA **PERVS** AT THIS BEACH HOUSE.

MUNCH MUNCH

BA-DUMP

BA-DUMP

....

PER-FECT.

HUFF...

HUFF...

TAKOYAKI BAR

MAYBE WE OUGHTA HAVE **BOOZE**, TOO.

CHAT

CHAT

I'LL CLAIM A BEARY LARGE SPACE, SO HALF WILL BE A REST AREA.

TAKE THAT **OFF** AL-READY.

SHAKA SHAKA

A BAR...

MIKU-SAN, I DON'T WANNA GO HOME...

AND TOP-QUALITY SAKE, *JUST* FOR YOU.

YOUR TAKO-YAKI.

STRESSFUL ALREADY, BUT HERE WE GO!

WHAT'S WRONG?!

M-MIKU-CHAN!

SWOON

SHOWING OFF THE CHARMS

OOOH!

JINGLE

SORRY TO KEEP YOU WAIT!

TH-THANK YOU!

MEYKO-CHAN, REAL CUTE!

NERU-CHAN, SO MOE!

AHA?

ANN-CHAN, TOO MUCH!

D-DON'T THINK YOU CAN JUST (ETC.) ...!

I GET THAT A LOT.

GLOOOOM

HAKU-SAN... IT, UH, SUITS YOU.

WHERE'RE YOUR FEET ...?

THE LEGEND BEGINS

STEP RIGHT UP! WE DON'T BITE!

THE VOCALO STALL OPENS!

MIYOYAKI 500円

TAKOYAKI 500円

COMIN' RIGHT UP! IT'S OUR SPECIALTY FLAVOR!

A MILLION YEN.

ONE, PLEASE.

YUMMMM!

AND VOCALO TAKOYAKI BECAME A NEW LEGEND.

SO GOOD!

OOH!

SPEAKS WITH HIS EYES

IT'S JUST ME AND LEN-KYUN!

LEN-KYUN...? CHOCO-LATE BANANAS?

STAAARE

DROOL

STAAARE

HE'S TOO CUTE!

CHOCOLATE

COMING RIGHT UP.

POINT

STAAARE

I'LL TAKE THE BIGGEST, TASTIEST CHOCO-LATE BANANA YOU'VE GOT!

SPRING ONION 11:
HACHUNE MIKU'S FESTIVAL SIDE B

PERFORMER'S SOUL

LUSTY LOCATION

MAY I HAVE...

THANK YOU

COURAGE

SEEING OFF

GOOD ENOUGH

DÉJÀ VU

MY PHONE... IT'S GONE!

HUH?

THE DEPARTMENT STORE ROOF, DAYS LATER.

CLACK

WHAT SHOULD I DO? I MESSED UP AGAIN...

IT COULDN'T BE... LEN-KYUN?!

WHIRL

GYAAH?!

NERU-SAAAN.

YOUR PHOOONE.

BUT SHE TOOK IT ANYWAY

WE'RE HOOOME!

TROMP

TROMP

IT'S NICE TO BE HOME.

FEELS LIKE WE'VE BEEN GONE A **WHILE**, HUH?

HUP!

I'LL PUT THESE AWAY.

TH-THAT'S TRUE.

GLANCE

WHAT FUN! MANY MEMORIES, NO?

WHA?! ANN-SAN, WHEN DID YOU TAKE THAT?!

BLUSH

WOULD MEY-SAN LIKE A SUMMER MEMENTO?

ANOTHER REUNION

THIS IS THE PLACE...

OH.

BA-DUMP

HUH? HAKU AND NERU?

HI

WELCOME! IT'S NICE TO SEE YOU!

AH! TSUNDERE MOE!

I-I DIDN'T COME TO SEE LEN-KYUN!

COME ON IN! I WANTED TO INVITE YOU, IN FACT.

TH-THANKS...

MIKU-SAN, I MISSED YOU...

SNIFF.

DON'T CRY! YOU'RE ALL SNOTTY!

CHATTER CHATTER

HAKU'S TRUE POWER

WELL...

HERE.

YOU'RE STILL SCARY IN THE DAYTIME.

TH-THANKS. WHY ARE YOU EVEN HERE?

SAY SOMETHING NEXT TIME.

I SAW YOU, SO I FOLLOWED YOU AWHILE.

HUH? HOW'D YOU GET THE ADDRESS?

DO YOU WANT TO COME...?

I WANTED TO VISIT VOCALOID MANOR.

I-I SEE.

NOOO, STOO-OOP!

TELL ME WHERE MIKU-NEESAN LIVES, OR I'LL HAUNT YOU OUTSIDE YOUR WINDOW EVERY NIGHT.

I JUST ASKED THE MANAGER.

I ALMOST FEEL BAD FOR HIM...

EASY, RIGHT?

THE TSUNDERE CATGIRL IN LOVE WITH LEN-KUN.

AKITA NERU

A slender blonde girl with a tsundere personality, usually found posting something on the Internet with her phone. She fell in love with Len at first sight but won't admit her feelings. When surprised, she becomes very catlike.

NYA!

HAPPY FACE?

ANGRY?

NARROWED EYES

CAT EYES

THE NEGATIVE WALLFLOWER GIRL

YOWANE HAKU

SURPRISED

HUH?

PANIC

I CAN'T DO IT!

NORMAL STATE

I'M SORRY ...

UH, HAPPY ....?

WEH !...

HA-CHUNE-SAN!...

SIGH...

IN ANY CASE...

She seems grown up and a little glamorous, but she's often drunk and always whining feebly or being masochistic. She has the weakest presence in the group and is the only female Vocaloid who wears long pants.

THE FOREIGN OTAKU VOCALOID

SWEET ANN

Music instructor by day, Protector of the Peace by night. When she first met Miku and the others, she was living in a tube at the park, for some reason.

AND SUPER-RARE KEYBOARD CRUSHER 1/8TH FIGURE!

I AM HAP-PIEST EVER!

A prototypical otaku, her passion for figurines and anime is something to behold. Her collection is so big that she could hold a one-person anime convention.

THE BIZARRE EUROPEAN DANDY

LEON

The manager of Crypt, the restaurant where Neru worked part-time. He seems to have some off-putting interests, so Miku sees him as an enemy.

MAIS OUI, IF IT ISN'T MIKU-SAN!

GAH! I'VE BEEN SPOTTED BY THE MANAGER PERV!!

Born in England. From his mannerisms to his chest hair, there's no doubt he embraces his European heritage wholeheartedly. Being scolded by Miku seems to make him happy?!

FINAL BOSS WHO MOON-LIGHTS AS A MANAGER

BEAR

He first appeared as the final boss in a virtual RPG game, but since then he's made random appearances.

IF A COUPLE WATCHES THE FIRE-WORKS THERE, THEIR LOVE WILL BEAR FRUIT.

I DON'T KNOW BEAR IT IS, THOUGH.

THERE'S A SECRET PLACE ON A HILL WITH A GREAT VIEW. THEY SAY...

TWITCH

Large, but timid; he cracks under pressure and gives in to puppy-dog eyes easily. Rumor has it that he's a very good singer.

GROWTH PERIOD

SPRING ONION 12: HACHUNE MIKU'S PART-TIME JOB

HUGE DAMAGE

BIG NEWS

DECLARATION

MORE BIG NEWS

OF COURSE

NICE TO MEET YOU?

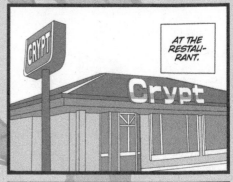

EVERY LIGHT HAS ITS SHADOW

ON PURPOSE?

TAKE-OUT

WHAT KIND OF CUSTOMER ARE YOU?!

AFTER HER SHIFT, THEN...

I HOPE HAKU-SAN DIDN'T **KIDNAP** HER!

JING-A-LING

I WONDER HOW MIKU-CHAN'S DOING.

HUFF HUFF

WHOA!

SLIDE

IS SHE OKAY ...?

NO.

FLAT-OUT

TAKE-OUT, PLEASE ...

SERVICE

MIKU-SAN. AH...

YEAH, SHE'S A REGULAR.

HAKU-SAN...

HUFF HUFF

WELL, WHEN-EVER YOU'RE READY.

MENU

STARE

MENU

OUR RESTAURANT DOESN'T OFFER *THAT* KIND OF SERVICE.

I'D LIKE MIKU-SAN, PLEASE.

SHE CAN DO IT

ROOM FOR IMPROVEMENT

YOU HAVEN'T GOTTEN THE HANG OF THINGS HERE YET!

ANYWAY, *VOUS* THERE!

H-HUH?!

POINT!

MOE, THAT *IS*!

I KNOW I'M A KLUTZ, BUT I'LL DO MY BEST...

I-I'M VERY SORRY.

DROOP

A TSUN-DERE? NOT WORKING POUR MOI!

A CLUMSY GIRL?

TWITCH

YOUR CHARACTER IS *TRÈS* CLICHÉ!

THAT THERE'S *MASO-CHISM*, PERV!!

HA HA HA!

......

NERU-KUN'S SCOLDING IS THE BEST MOE, OUI! OUI!!

THE MANAGER ARRIVES

PEEK

IS EVERYONE WORKING HARD, *S'IL VOUS PLAIT*?

MANAGER LEON!

AHA!

HE DESIGNED THE UNI-FORMS!

REALLY?

HO HO.

STEP

?!

FLUTTER~ ♡

I *TOLD* YOU NOT TO COME OUT LIKE THAT!

SHOOM

A-HA!

BOOONG

WHAT IN THE HECK?

MOMENT OF BLISS

SHOW OF DETERMINATION

RIN'S REVIVAL?

RIN-SAAAN! THERE'S A **SCOUT** HERE FOR YOU.

HUH? A SCOUT?

HUH? AW, **SHUCKS.**

BLUSH

IT'S WAT.

YOU'RE ADORABLE! WE **MUST** HAVE YOU!

FAMOUS?!

HEH HEH HEH.

YOU COULD BE **FAMOUS!**

I HEAR YOU! I **HEAR** YOU, **ARRIGHT?!**

BUT CAN YOU COME BACK NOW?

SORRY TO INTERRUPT YOUR **DAYDREAM.**

TAP

THE CHOSEN PEOPLE

NOW HIRING

PEOPLE OF CRYPT! YOUR BELOVED MANAGER IS **DEAD!**

HAH HAH HAH...

TWITCH

TWITCH

OOOH!

THIS RESTAURANT IS NOW UNDER MY CONTROL!

NOW **RISE,** MY PEOPLE!

FIRST, **ANYONE** IS ALLOWED TO WEAR THE UNIFORM!

KYAAAA!!

ALL HAIL MIKU!

ALL HAIL MIKU!

TREMBLE

TREMBLE

TREMBLE

ALL HAIL MIKU!

TOO POWERFUL

MIKU-CHAN! STOP THIS TYRANNY AT ONCE!

STOMP

SAY THAT... TO THIS?!

URK! YOU...!

I'M A MOE-MOE CUTE GAL, TOO.

Y'KNOW...

AND THIS?!

I-I WON'T GIVE IN!

THEN HOW ABOUT THIS!

THIS DO IT FOR YOU, LOLI-CON?

AAH! YOU WIN!!

THROB

SHE SAID IT

WE'RE RUNNING OUT OF FOOD.

BOSS MIKU...

OUT OF DESSERT, TOO! CAKE IS GONE!

TWIRL

SO? WHO CARES?

DUN-DUN

IF THEY HAVE NO CAKE, LET THEM EAT SPRING ONIONS.

EPILOGUE

PAPARAZZI

JUST CAN'T QUIT

SHIINING BRIIIGHTLY ...♪

IN MEYKO'S ROOM.

WHOA, YOU'RE RIGHT!

OOOH.

MIKU-CHAN, AREN'T YOU IN CHARGE OF DINNER?

HMMMM...

YOU BLEW UP LIKE A **BALLOON**! HA HA!

I GAINED WEIGHT FROM TOO MANY SPRING ONIONS, SO I GOTTA BE CAREFUL.

SO MUCH FOR BEING CAREFUL.

I'VE GOT IT! LET'S HAVE SPRING ONION HOTPOT!

LOOKING FORWARD TO LATER

VOCALO SHOPPING DISTRICT.

GOOD!

VOCALO SHOPPING DISTRICT

CHATTER CHATTER

BUSTLE BUSTLE

CHEAP?

OPENING SALE

OH! HI, MIKU-CHAN!

WATCH SHOP 3

WHAT'RE YOU DOING, KAIYTO-N!?

OOH...

HM.

THERE'S A SPECIAL ICE CREAM TODAY, BUT I COULDN'T RESERVE IT, SO I'M WAITING IN LINE.

YEAH, THANKS! SEE YOU LATER.

GOOD LUCK.

WELL, HOPE YOU GET SOME!

WAVE WAVE

NOT SO BAD

I'M ON IT!

FWIP

BUY INGREDIENTS BESIDES SPRING ONIONS, PLEASE!

HUH? YOU CAN'T TAKE MORE RESERVA-TIONS?

PHEW.

WAH, THIS SUCKS.

BOO-HOO...

BUT THAT'S NOT SO BAD.

I HAD TO BEG THEM TO SAVE ME A FEW...

HOLY PILGRIMAGE

HMM?

Spring Onion Specialty Shop

BA

NOW OPEN

BETTER GET SPRING ONIONS FIRST...

WHEN DID THIS SHOP OPEN?!

A SPRING ONION SPECIALTY SHOP?! O.M.G.!

OOOOOH!!

YOU'RE BEARY WELCOME!

DASH

LET US ENTER THIS EL DORADO!

SPRING ONION PARADISE

FREEZE!

BEARY... FINAL BOSS?

OFFICIAL BUSINESS

OH! MIKU-CHAN!

HOBBY SHOP

ANN-SAN!

NO TIME FOR WORK! THERE IS LIMITED-EDITION FIGURE OUT!

OH HO HO!

IT'S A WEEK-DAY.

YOU'RE NOT WORKING TODAY?

EVEN IF SOMETHING HAPPENS...

YOU'RE THE WORST ADULT EVER.

.....

TSK! TSK!

Eco-Eco Bag

THIS IS STUDENT AP-PROVED?!

CALO MUSIC SCHOOL

SENSEEE!

CLASS-ROOM IS RIGHT THERE, SO ALL IS OKAY!

OUT OF BOUNDS

AH...!

PLEASE PUT YOUR BEAR HAND AWAY.

THE BEACH HOUSE CAN'T BEAR STAYING OPEN ALL YEAR. SO I STARTED THIS...

MIKU LIFE

MILLION VOLT EYES

WE SEE EACH OTHER ALL THE **TIME.**

GRAB

SHUDDER SHUDDER

MIKU-NEESAN! I **MISSED** YOU...!!

YOU'RE **CREEPY,** HAKU.

AT FIRST, I WAS PRE-BEARED TO OPEN A FRUIT STAND, BUT...

I WAS ACTUALLY BEARY RELUC-TANT, BUT...

WE DECIDED ON A SPRING ONION STORE FOR YOUR SAKE.

OOH!

MIKU LIFE

SET MY HEART ON FIRE

STOP CALLING ME FINAL BOSS! I CAN'T *BEAR* IT!

FINAL BOSS... WHAT'RE *YOU* DOING HERE?

SO CLOSE TO OUR HOUSE...

YOU'RE MY BEARY FIRST CUSTOMER, MIKU-SAN.

I'M SUR-PRISED, THOUGH!

REVENGE

A SPRING ONION SPECIALTY STORE...

RMB RMB RMB RMB

AND IT'S REALLY ...

WHAT KIND OF BEARFACED DEMAND IS *THAT?!*

BWAAAN

GIVE ME THIS SHOP!

HEAD

NATURAL ENEMIES

NEXT IS ORANGES AND BANANAS.

ALL RIGHTY.

FREE

OPEN TODAY! THE CRYPTO FRUIT SHOP FOR ALL YOUR ORANGE AND BANANA NEEDS!

THE BANANAS MIGHT BE SOLD OUT...

CRYPTO FRUIT SHOP

OPEN

OPEN

DUN-DUUUN

I'VE GOT A **BAD** FEELING ABOUT THIS.

YIKES...

CLOSING UP SHOP

WHITE ONIONS, GREEN ONIONS, SHIMONITA ONIONS, OH MY!

OOH, MOUNTAIN ONIONS!

OOH!

WHOA!

BOY, YOU REALLY WENT **ALL** OUT.

WE GOT ALL THE SPRING ONIONS WE COULD FIND, NEESAN.

HEH HEH!

PLEASE! TAKE **WHATEVER** YOU WANT!

OKAY, WHAT TO BUY ...

THIS, THIS...

ON THE HOUSE

HEY, W--!

HUFF, HUFF...

WE'LL GO OUT OF **BEARS-NESS** LIKE THAT!!

FOR YOU, IT'LL ALL BE FREE FOR LIFE!!

FRONT-ROW SEATS

SNEEEAK

BIEN-VENUE? DON'T TELL ME...

BIENVENUE! YES, WELCOME!

SPRING ONION 13:
HACHUNE MIKU'S MISSION SIDE B

CAN-DO!

SinPully Delicious

AH HAAN.

AH...

THESE FRUITS ARE NOT JUST **CHEAP**, BUT *TRÈS* SPECIAL!

THOSE OTHER SHOPS CAN'T COMPARE, NON!

TAKE THIS APPLE!

UH-OH. THOSE TWO KIDS AT THE FRONT...

GDG

EEK!

GOT ANY ORANGES FOR TASTE-TESTIN', MISTER?

GREAT MINDS THINK ALIKE

NATURALLY GIFTED

LIGHT AND DARKNESS

THE BOSS'S REQUEST

HIGH SPEED

THAT'S OUR MANAGER

FLAVORTOWN

EH HEH.

THERE'RE **SIDE DISHES,** TOO!

TA-DA! IT'S MIKU-CHAN'S SPECIAL SPRING ONION HOTPOT!

OOH, LOOKS PRETTY **GOOD!**

BUBBLE BUBBLE

WE WILL CALL IT "MIKU HOTPOT," NO?

IT'S ONLY SPRING ONIONS, BUT IT'S STILL GOOD!

OOH, NICE AN' **NORMAL.**

JUST BONITO FLAKES.

WHAT'S IN THE **BROTH?**

WHAT'D YOU *THINK* IT WAS GONNA TASTE LIKE?

I TRIED TO MAKE BROTH OUT OF SPRING ONIONS, BUT IT DIDN'T REALLY WORK.

THESE THINGS HAPPEN

STOMP STOMP

MEY-CHAN! I'M STARV-IIIN'!

MIKU-CHAN'S IN CHARGE TODAY.

WHAT'S FOR DINNER?

WHA--?!

NOTHIN' BUT SPRING ONIONS AGAIN, *HUH?*

I *DO* FEEL A LITTLE BAD ABOUT THAT.

IT WAS A **MINCED ONION** BURGER, NOT A HAMBURGER.

THEY'RE FINE, BUT THE "SPRING ONION BURGERS" YOU MADE HAD BARELY ANY MEAT...

THE DREAM IS DEAD

THAT WAS SOME **GOOD** EATIN'.

WHEW.

MMM! I'M SO FULL!

OOF.

THAT'S RIGHT!

KAIYTO-NII'S IN CHARGE OF DINNER NEXT, RIGHT?

OOH!

I'LL HAVE TO WORK HARD SO I DON'T LOSE TO MIKU-CHAN!

DENIED!

MY DREAM ICE CREAM DINNER, OF COURSE!

WHAT WILL YOU MAKE?

TEARS OF GRATITUDE

OOOH!

WE'VE GOT **DESSERT** TONIGHT, TOO!

IT'S THE ONE I COULDN'T GET TODAY...!

THIS ICE CREAM!!

THIS...

TA-

Hagen Dutch

DA!

HUH, WOW.

HERE.

MEY-CHAN USED HER **WILES** TO RESERVE IT FOR YOU.

WEEP WEEP

HEE HEE HEE.

I-IT'S NOT LIKE I DID IT *JUST* FOR KAIYTO-KUN OR ANYTHING...

BLUUUSH

YUM!

THE KIDS WERE WATCHING

OH?

WHEW! THAT WAS A NICE BATH!

LOOKIN' GOOD AS USUAL TODAY.

OH YEAH.

HEH.

WHAT'S COOKIN', GOOD LOOKIN'? HA!

I'VE GOT IT GOIN' ON, LIKE ALWAYS...

CLATTER

AARGH!

GOLDEN RIGHT HOOK

WHY ARE YOU ALL SHOUTING...

WHAT'S GOING ON?

WAAAIT!

ERM...

LITTLE GIRLS (?)
⇓
CHASING
⇓
HALF-NAKED

DIVINE PUNISHMENT!!

天誅!!

KA-WHAM

IN A PICKLE

U-UM...

STARE

SLAM

SHWP

WHA--?!

WH--

MEY-CHAA-AAN.

PATTER PATTER PATTER

WAH!

OH NO, A PERV!!

W-W-WAAAAIT!!

FLASH ☆

GOLDEN RIGHT HOOK (AGAIN)

A BIG PICKLE

WHAT HAPPENED?

HUH?

WHA...?

I'M SAVING YOUR LIFE, MONSIEUR!

?!

HUFF

MY LIPS ARE IN DANGER?!

NON, IT'S A MISUNDERSTANDING!

GYAAAAAAAH!

NRHAVBNW234IVOASD!!!

DECISION

WH-WHAT JUST HAPPENED TO MOI...?

OH MY.

DIZZY

IT'S THAT LOLICON FROM BEFORE, NON?

OOH!

THIS ISN'T GOOD AT ALL, NON!

SHAKE

HE'S UNCONSCIOUS! EXCUSEZ-MOI!!

SHAKE

URGH...

I'M SURE HE MEANS WELL, BUT I CAN'T WATCH.

HUFF

HUFF

MAIS OUI, I'LL HAVE TO USE CPR!

DIVE   DÉJÀ VU

I SEE! SO *THAT'S* WHAT HAPPENED.

A LITTLE LATER.

I WONDER WHERE THEY WENT?

THEY'RE ALL TAKING A WHILE.

I WAS AT FAULT FOR HOW *I* ACTED, TOO.

GOSH, I'M SORRY FOR MIS-UNDER-STANDING.

FIDGET

I SHOULDN'T HAVE DONE THAT TO POOR KAIYTO-KUN...

· · · · · ·

BUT, UM...

HOW SHOULD I PUT THIS...?

OH, **THERE** THEY ARE.

WAAH! GYAAAH!

I'LL HAVE TO APOLO-GI--

OOPSIE!

I JUST WISH YOU'D REALIZED A LITTLE **SOONER**.

YOU SAID YOU WEREN'T SERIOUS... MEN ARE THE *WORST*.

MUMBLE

 01 ミラクルロケット39号

作詞・作曲：Otomania

まぶしい朝日に
元気良くあいさつをして
部屋から飛び出す　楽しい一日始まる

不思議な力が　宿るステッキの先っぽ
二つに束ねた　髪と同じ色してる

泣きそうな時は　上向いて歩こう
ほらごらん　どこまでも
晴れ渡る空　GO！

飛ばせ　飛ばせ　ミラクルロケット
世界中を萌葱（もえぎ）色に染めるわ

Sunny Day　Shiny Day
今日もいい天気
私が歩く道に雨なんて降らないわ

不思議な力が
宿るステッキをふりふり
みんなを元気にする
秘密のおまじない

悲しい気持ちなんて
すぐに消えちゃうから
ほらごらん　あたたかい
みんなの笑顔　GO！

進め　進め　ミラクルロケット
世界中を幸せで塗りつぶせ

Sunny Day　Shiny Day
今日もいい天気
私のハートには涙なんていらないわ

飛ばせ　飛ばせ　ミラクルロケット
世界中を萌葱（もえぎ）色に染めるわ

Sunny Day　Shiny Day
明日もいい天気
私が歩く道に雨なんて降らないわ

Miracle Rocket #39

Music and lyrics: Otomania

saying hello
to a bright morning
burst out of my room another fun day begins

a mysterious power rests inside this stick
the same color as my hair tied in two parts

if you feel like crying just look up
and walk forward see? it goes on forever
the cloudless sky GO!

fly, fly miracle rocket
dye the whole world the color of onions

Sunny Day   Shiny Day
the weather's great again today
it never rains on the path I'm walking

a mysterious power
rests inside the stick I wave around
making everyone happy
with a secret spell

sad feelings and such
will disappear in no time
see? they're so warm
everyone's smiles GO!

keep going, keep going miracle rocket
paint the whole world in happiness

Sunny Day   Shiny Day
the weather's great again today
there's no need for tears in my heart

fly, fly miracle rocket
dye the whole world the color of onions

Sunny Day   Shiny Day
the weather'll be great again tomorrow
it never rains on the path I'm walking

mabushii asahi ni
genki yoku aisatsu wo shite
heya kara tobidasu tanoshii ichinichi hajimaru

fushigi na chikara ga yadoru sutekki no sakippo
futatsu ni tabaneta kami to onaji iro shiteru

nakisou na toki wa ue muite arukou
hora goran dokomademo
harewataru sora GO!

tobase tobase mirakuru roketto
sekaijuu wo moegi iro ni someru wa

Sunny Day   Shiny Day
kyou mo ii tenki
watashi ga aruki michi ni amen ante furanai wa

fushigi na chikara ga
yadoru sutekki wo furifuri
minna wo genki ni suru
himitsu no omajinai

kanashii kimochi nante
sugu ni kiechau kara
horagoran atatatakai
minna no egao GO!

susume susume mirakuru roketto
sekaijuu wo shiawase de nuritsubuse

Sunny Day   Shiny Day
kyou mo ii tenki
watashi no haato ni wa namida nante iranai wa

tobase tobase mirakuru roketto
sekaijuu wo moegi iro ni someru wa

Sunny Day   Shiny Day
ashita mo ii tenki
watashi ga aruku michi ni amen ante furanai wa

Comeback Hill

Music and lyrics: Otomania

open my right hand stretch out my finger with that finger at the ready the usual stance	migite wo aite yubi nobashite sono yubi wo soroerya itsumo no kamae
oi oi nope nope why in the heck if you make a joke I'll have a comeback no matter what	oi oi chau chau nandeyanen boketara nandemo tsukkomu de
my life is all about wits I'll keep on climbing this comeback hill	uchi no jinsei kireaji inochi nobori tsudukeru tsukkomi saka
tightening the ribbon on my head so deliberately my partner approaches	atama no ribbon wo shimenaoshite jikkuri ukagau aite no dekata
oi oi nope nope what in the heck if you make a joke I'll have a comeback no matter when	oi oi chau chau donaiyanen boketara itsudemo tsukkomu de
my life is all about position I'll keep on climbing this comeback hill	uchi no jinsei tachiichi inochi nobori tsudukeru tsukkomi saka
there are only two kinds of people in this world ones who joke and ones who make comebacks	kono yo ni hito wa futatoori dake bokeru yaku ka tsukkomu yaku ka
oi oi nope nope oh, whatever if you make a joke I'll have a comeback no matter where	oi oi chau chau mou ee nen boketara dokodemo tsukkomu de
my life is all about a clenched fist I'll keep on climbing this comeback hill	uchi no jinsei uraken inochi nobori tsudukeru tsukkomi saka

02 つっこみ坂

作詞・作曲：Otomania

右手を開いて　指伸ばして
その指揃えりゃ　いつもの構え

おいおい　ちゃうちゃう
なんでやねん
ボケたら　何でも
つっこむで

ウチの人生　切れ味命
のぼり続ける　つっこみ坂

頭のリボンを　締め直して
じっくりうかがう　相手の出方

おいおい　ちゃうちゃう
どないやねん
ボケたら　いつでも
つっこむで

ウチの人生　立ち位置命
のぼり続ける　つっこみ坂

この世に人は　二通りだけ
ボケる役か　つっこむ役か

おいおい　ちゃうちゃう
もうええねん
ボケたら　どこでも
つっこむで

ウチの人生　裏拳命
のぼり続ける　つっこみ坂

04 はちゅねミク音頭
〜はちゅね顔の絵描き歌〜
作詞・作曲：hmixt

まるいお皿に

まるい輪が二つ

その下　三角形一つおいて

渦巻き模様を左右に並べ

その上　蕎麦の棒

左右に置くよ

お皿の両側に

緑の葉が落ちて

赤いかまぼこ二つ

葉っぱにのせてみる

頭にも葉をのせ

ネギを添えたら

出来たお顔は「はちゅねミク」

03 はちゅねのうずまき
〜ぐるぐるほっぺのすごい奴〜
作詞・作曲：mirumiru

ねーぎ！

ぐるぐるほっぺのすごい奴
はちゅねまして　はちゅねミク

ぐるぐる渦巻きまわってる
目がまわるよ　　はちゅねミク

ぐるぐるぐるぐる…（YO！YO！）
はちゅねのぐるぐる〜
ぐるぐるぐるぐる…（YO！YO！）
はちゅねのうずまき〜

ねーぎ！

ぐるぐるほっぺの癒し系
愛されキャラ　　はちゅねミク

ぐるぐるネギをまわして
みんな一緒に　　はちゅねミク

ぐるぐるぐるぐる…（YO！YO！）
はちゅねのぐるぐる〜
ぐるぐるぐるぐる…（YO！YO！）
はちゅねのうずまき〜

ねーぎ！

05 NeGi boogie
作詞・作曲：まいと

NeGi boogie
〜spring onion boogie〜
Music and lyrics: maito

03 The Hachune Spiral
~the awesome twirling cheeks~
Music and lyrics: mirumiru

spring onion!	neegi!
the awesome twirls on my cheeks nice to hachune meet you hachune miku	guruguru hoppe no sugoi yatsu hachunemashite hachune miku
the twirling spirals spin your eyes will spin too hachune miku	guruguru uzumaki mawatteru me ga mawaru yo hachune miku
twirl twirl... (YO! YO!) the hachune twirl~ twirl twirl... (YO! YO!) the hachune spiral~	guruguru guruguru... (YO! YO!) hachune no guruguru~ guruguru guruguru... (YO! YO!) hachune no uzumaki~
spring onion!	neegi!
the healing twirls on my cheeks beloved character hachune miku	guruguru hoppe no iyashikei aisare kyarahachune miku
twirling a spring onion all together now hachune miku	guruguru negi wo mawashite minna issho ni hachune miku
twirl twirl... (YO! YO!) the hachune twirl~ twirl twirl... (YO! YO!) the hachune spiral~	guruguru guruguru... (YO! YO!) hachune no guruguru~ guruguru guruguru... (YO! YO!) hachune no uzumaki~
spring onion!	neegi!

04 Hachune Miku's March
~the drawing Hachune's face song~
Music and lyrics: hmixt

make a round plate with two round rings below themadd one triangle line up spiral shapes to the left and right above themadd sticks of soba to the left and right	marui osara ni marui wa ga futatsu sono shita sankakukei hitotsu oite uzumaki moyou wo sayuu ni narabe sono ue soba no bou sayuu ni oku yo
on either side of the plate two green leaves fall then two red kamaboko place one on each leaf put a leaf on the head too now add a spring onion and the face you've made is "hachune miku"	osara no ryougawa ni midori no ha ga ochite akai kamaboko futatsu happa ni nosetemiru atama ni mo ha wo nose negi wo soetara dekita okao wa "hachune miku"

06 ☆the PaPoPuPi of love☆
Lyrics: ☆μκëy☆ Music: WEB-MIX

papupipipupo popupipipu
papupipipupopepo papupipipu

chiisana tsukue naranda kyoushitsu
de kimi itsumo (wa!!)
ikinari ooki na koe deatashi odokasu no

yobarete furumitara punitto
hoppe ga hekonda (nmou!!)

"doushite…?"
sonna koto bakkari de.
kotae wakannai
demo ne guruguru guruguru kangaetetara
nandakanda soba ni
ite kureta no wa kimi data

korette moshikashite ano
koi tte iu yatsu nano nee? (nn?)
attakakute sukoshi kurushikute
amai no ni suppakute
korokoro kuchi no naka de dansu suru
doroppu mitai (un!)

me tojitemo pasuteru no sekai ga
oku ni hirogaru suki to ka koi to ka
yoku wakannai kedo
nandakanda atashi wa kimi to issho ni itai

popupopi popipapu
popopipa pupepopo pu
popipapi papupopo
pipapupe popopupo pi
papipapupopopipa
pupepopa pupopipa pi
papupopo pipapupe
popapupo pipapipa pu
aaaaaaaaaaa

kimi to no kisu wa donna a-ji? (chu?)

papupipipupo popupipipu
papupipipupopepo papupipipu

small desks lined up in the classroom
you always (wah!!)
shout out suddenly startling me

when you called to me, I turned around
and, squish, my cheek got poked (ugh!!)

"why…?"
it's always like this.
I don't know the answer
but you know, when I really thought hard about it
I realized somehow you're the person
who's always by my side

this couldn't possibly be
that thing called love, is it? (hmm?)
warm, slightly painful
sweet yet sour
like a roly-poly drop that dances
in your mouth (yep!)

even when I close my eyes, a pastel world
spreads all around "like" and "love"
I don't know much about that stuff
But I somehow want to be with you

popupopi popipapu
popopipa pupepopo pu
popipapi papupopo
pipapupe popopupo pi
papipapupopopipa
pupepopa pupopipa pi
papupopo pipapupe
popapupo pipapipa pu
aaaaaaaaaaa

what would a kiss with you ta-ste like? (mwah?)

☆恋のPaPoPuPi☆

作詞：☆μκëy☆ 作曲：WEB-MIX

ぱぷぴぴぷぽ　ぱぷぴぴぷ
ぱぷぴぴぷぽぺぱ　ぱぷぴぴぷ

小さな机並んだ　教室で君いつも（わっ‼）
いきなり大きな声で　あたし脅かすの

呼ばれて振り向いたらプニっと
ほっぺがへこんだ（んもぅ‼）

『どうして…？』
そんなことばっかりで。
答えわかんない
でもね　グルグルグルグル　考えてたら
なんだかんだ傍に
いてくれたのは君だった

これって　もしかしてあの
恋っていうやつなのねぇ？（ん？）
あったかくて少し苦しくて
甘いのに酸っぱくて
コロコロ　口の中でダンスする
ドロップみたい（うん！）

目閉じてもパステルの世界が
奥に広がる　好きとか恋とか
よくわかんないけど
なんだかんだあたしは君と一緒にいたい

ぱぷぽぴ　ぱぴぱぷ
ぽぽぴぱ　ぷぺぽぱ　ぷ
ぽぴぱぴ　ぱぷぽぽ
ぴぱぷぺ　ぽぱぷぽ　ぴ
ぱぴぱぷ　ぽぽぴぱ
ぷぺぽぱ　ぷぽぴぱ　ぴ
ぱぷぽぽ　ぴぱぷぺ
ぽぱぷぽ　ぴぱぴぱ　ぷ
あああああああああああ

君とのキスはどんなあ〜じ？(チュ?)

AFTERWORD

Ahem... Hello there. I'm Otomania of "Ontama." I hope you enjoyed *LoiPara* Volume 1! Thank you very much for reading all the way to the end.

Tamago-san and I came up with Hachune Miku while we were just goofing off. She's gone from being a random joke to having her own manga, something we never could've imagined a year ago. For the two of us, who didn't even know the first kanji in the word "manga," every day (including this very moment) has been a learning experience. Looking back, this year has gone by in a flash. I hope you'll all continue enjoying the adventures of Hachune and her friends.

I want to thank Wat-san and Crypton-san for making Hachune Miku official, and our reassuring editor Sadamatsu-san for kindly looking after us as we fumbled along. Morino Aruji-san, among others, gave us lots of advice about manga. Please allow me to thank all the many other people who helped us out, too. Thank you for everything!

Finally, the biggest thanks of all goes to everyone who loves Hachune Miku and the LoiPara family.

SEVEN SEAS ENTERTAINMENT PRESENTS

Hachune Miku's Everyday Vocaloid Paradise!

story and art by ONTAMA

VOLUME 1

TRANSLATION
Jenny McKeon

ADTAPTATION
Rebecca Scoble
Lianne Sentar

LETTERING AND RETOUCH
Rina Mapa

COVER DESIGN
Nicky Lim

PROOFREADER
Shanti Whitesides
Tom Speelman

ASSISTANT EDITOR
Jenn Grunigen

PRODUCTION ASSISTANT
CK Russell

PRODUCTION MANAGER
Lissa Pattillo

EDITOR-IN-CHIEF
Adam Arnold

PUBLISHER
Jason DeAngelis

HACHUNE MIKU NO NICHIJO ROIPARA! VOLUME 1
© ONTAMA 2009
© Crypton Future Media, INC. www.piapro.net **piapro**
First published in Japan in 2009 by KADOKAWA CORPORATION, Tokyo.
English translation rights arranged with KADOKAWA CORPORATION, Tokyo
through TOHAN CORPORATION, Tokyo.

Seven Seas books may be purchased in bulk for promotional, educational, or business use. Please contact your local bookseller or the Macmillan Corporate and Premium Sales Department at 1-800-221-7945, extension 5442, or by e-mail at MacmillanSpecialMarkets@macmillan.com.

Seven Seas and the Seven Seas logo are trademarks of Seven Seas Entertainment, LLC. All rights reserved.

ISBN: 978-1-626926-15-8

Printed in Canada

First Printing: October 2017

10 9 8 7 6 5 4 3 2 1

FOLLOW US ONLINE: www.gomanga.com

READING DIRECTIONS

This book reads from *right to left*, Japanese style. If this is your first time reading manga, you start reading from the top right panel on each page and take it from there. If you get lost, just follow the numbered diagram here. It may seem backwards at first, but you'll get the hang of it! Have fun!!

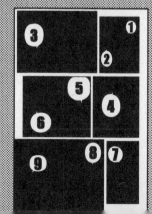